Jesus Wants to Spend Time with YOU!

Written By
Brandi & Robyn Cunningham
Fireside Grace

Jesus Wants to Spend Time with You!
Copyright 2023 by Brandi and Robyn Cunningham

All rights reserved. No part of this book may be reproduced, stored in a retrieval system, or transmitted in any form or by any means-electronic, mechanical, photocopy, recording, or otherwise-without prior written permission of the copyright owner. All emphasis in Scripture quotations are author's own.

All scripture quotations are taken from the Amplified® Bible (AMP), Copyright © 2015 by The Lockman Foundation. Used by permission.

ISBNs: 978-1-953143-06-8 (Paperback)

  978-1-953143-02-0 (Ebook)

Printed in the U.S.A.

To my firstborn, Asher, who loves robots and whose love language is quality time. This one's for you, Bud!

Did you know,

God created all of the world....

Because He wants to spend time with you?

Did you know,

God created the water, land, and houses

all because He wants to spend time with you?

Did you know,

That Father God gave up the most precious thing He ever had, His son Jesus...

because He wants to spend time with you?

Did you know,

that Jesus gave up His perfect home in heaven to go through the worst and most terrible things,

All because He wants to spend time with you?

Did you know,

that nothing you ever do can change the fact that God wants to spend time with you? Nothing you could do, and not even the seasons that change.

Did you know,

all you have to do to spend time with God is simply talk to Him like you would to me.

That's all you have to do.

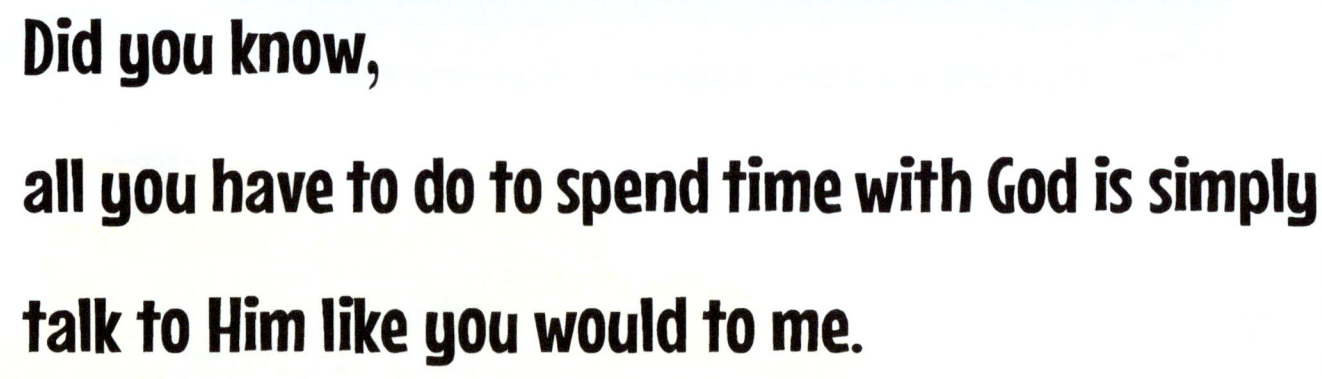

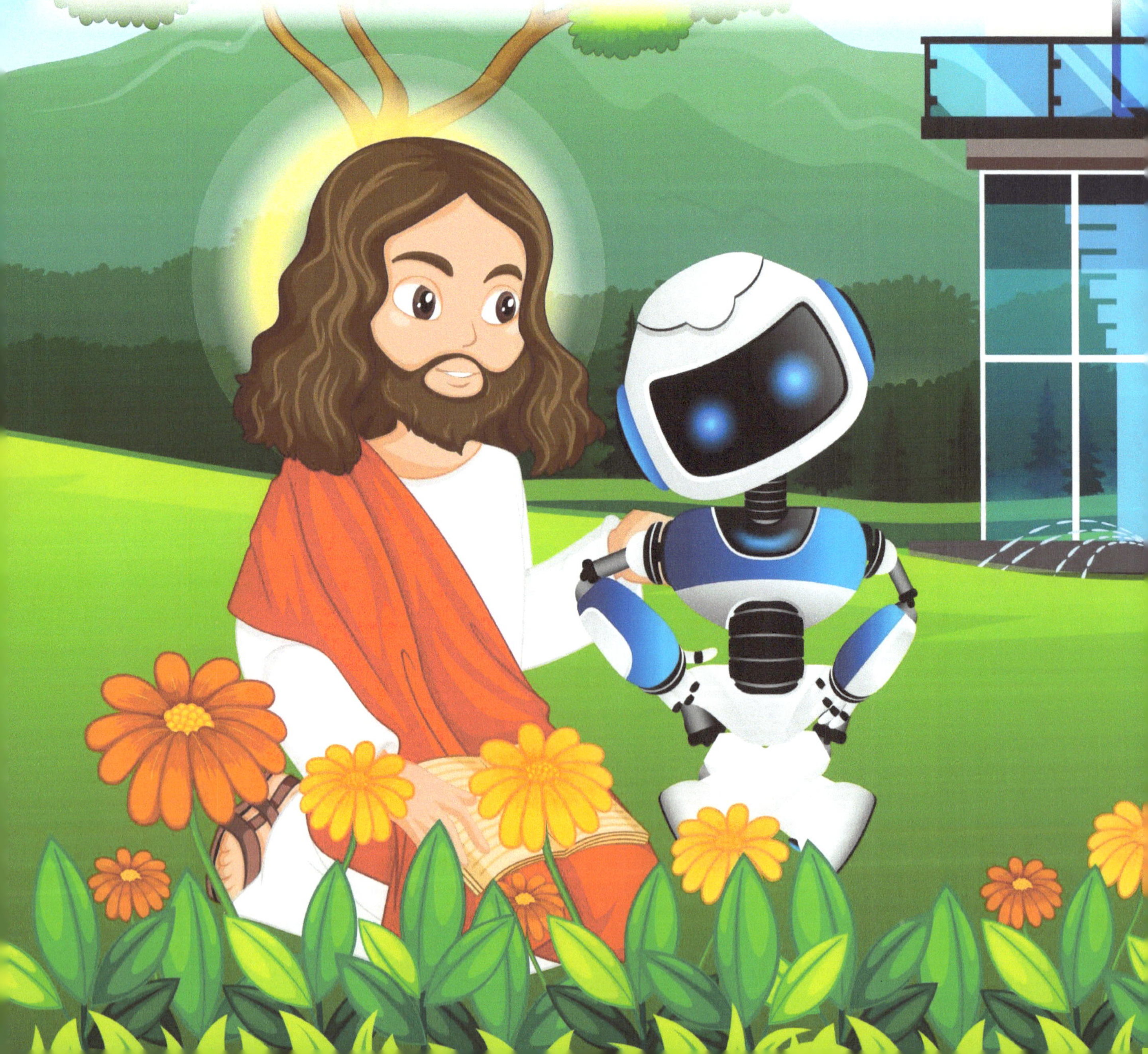

That you are precious, wanted, called, chosen, special, set apart, appreciated, and loved,

More than the birds in the air,

The fish in the sea,

More than any problem that will ever be.

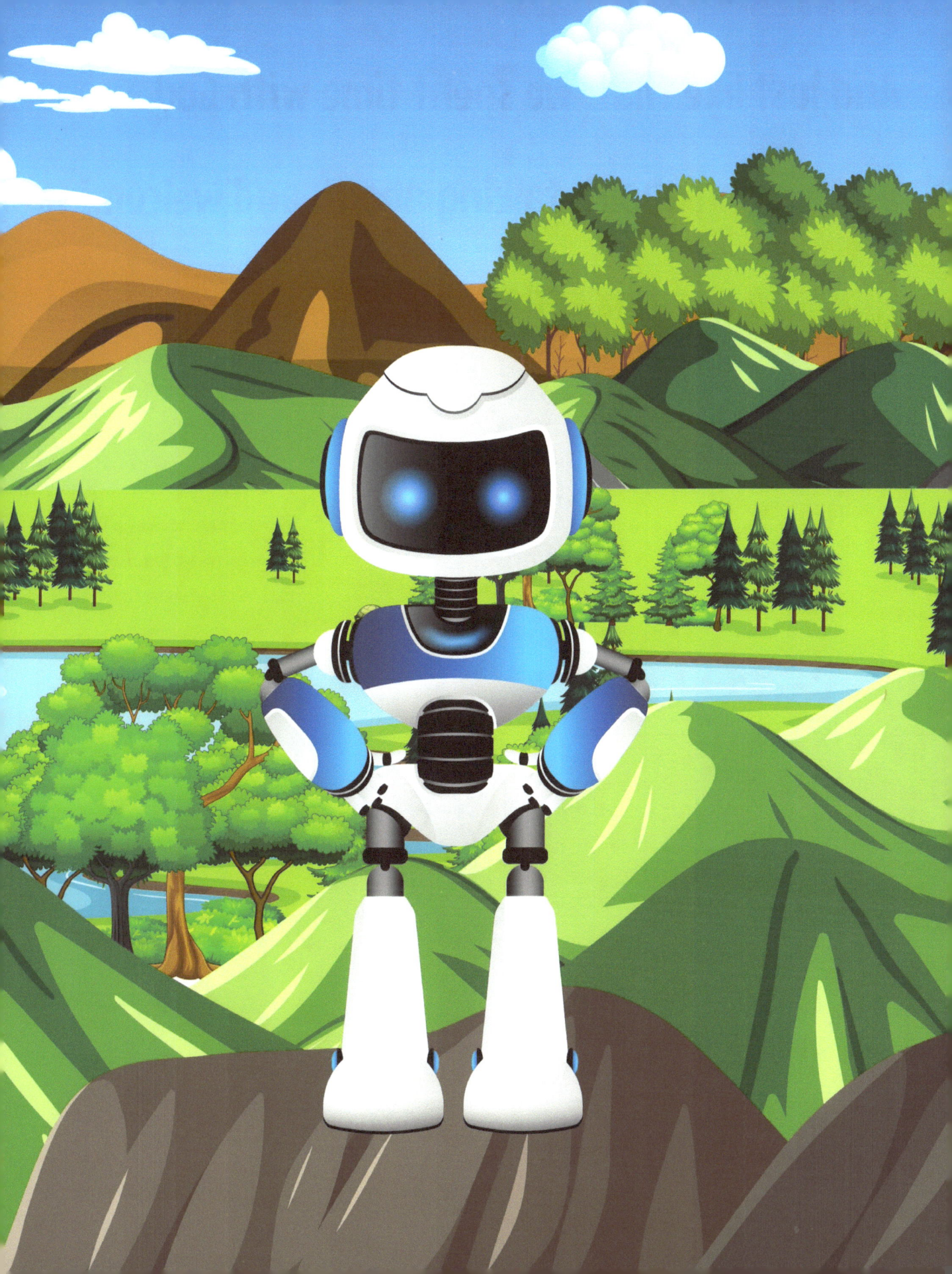

And just like that, we spent time with God by thinking about, talking about, and welcoming Him into our talk today.

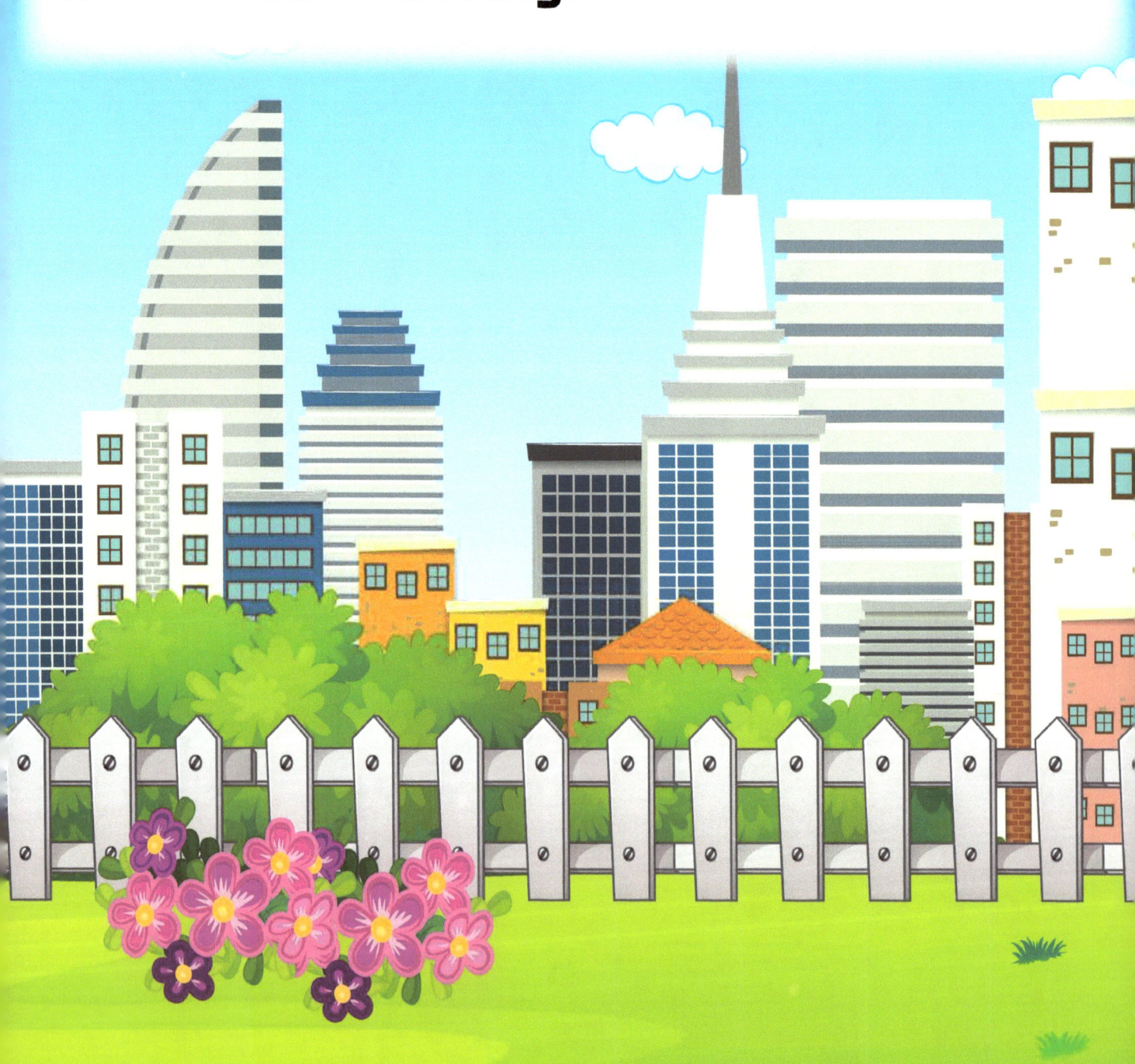

Go be who you were created to be,

spending time with God,

who loves you more than anything in the sea.

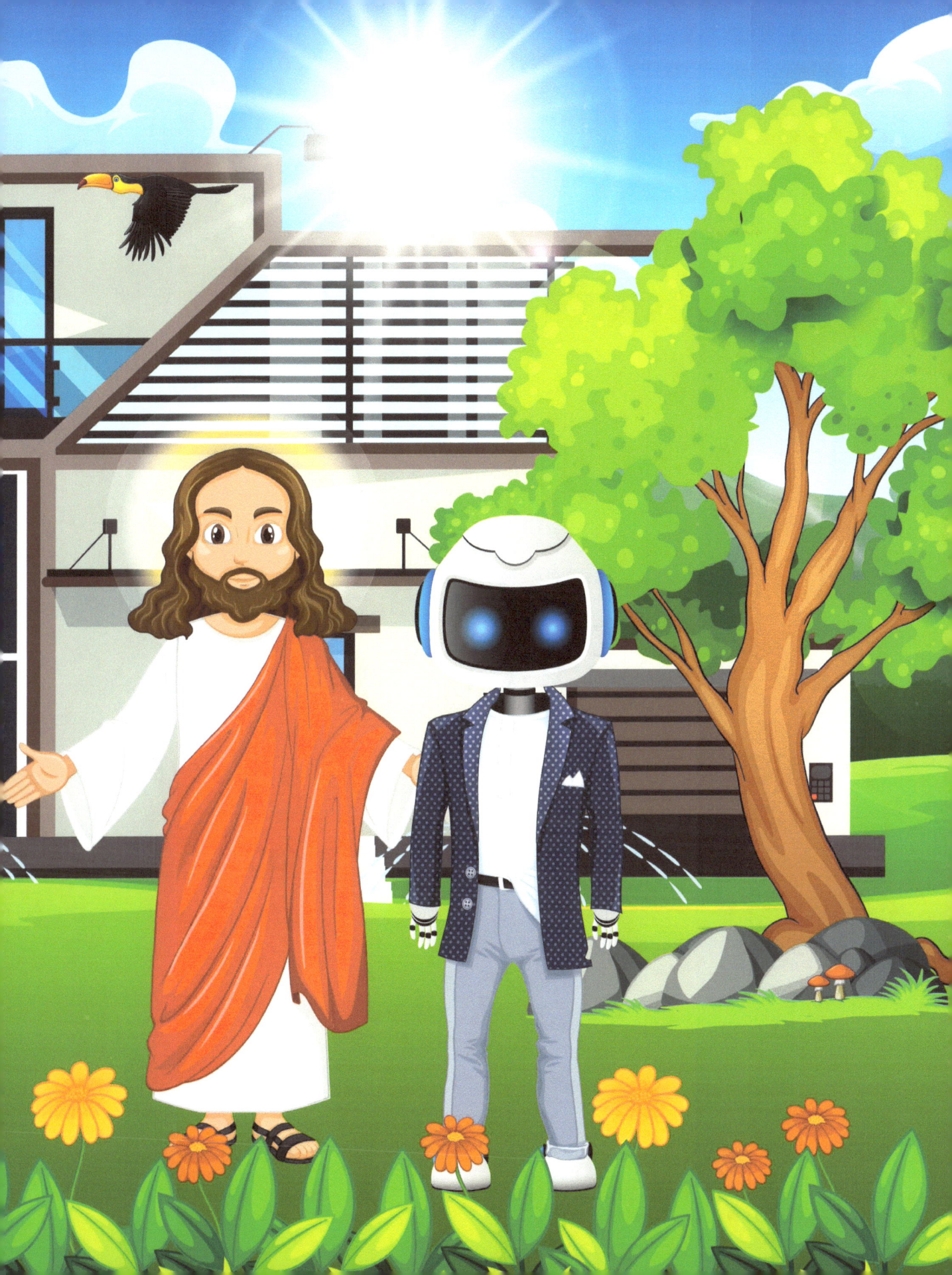

Scripture memory verses: Deuteronomy 14:2

You have been set apart as holy to the LORD your God, and he has chosen you from all the nations of the earth to be his own special treasure.

Song of Solomon 2:10

My beloved spoke, and said to me, "Rise up, my love, my beautiful one, and come away."

About Brandi and Robyn Cunningham

Robyn and Brandi Cunningham are the founders of Fireside Grace, which was birthed to help individuals, ministries, and cities live to their full potential through Christ-based discipleship. Using the gifts of the Spirit, they teach truth to bring clarity to the body of Christ on issues that seem confusing in this modern age. Robyn and Brandi are ordained under Michael French with Patria Ministries. They have been involved with various areas of ministry for the last ten years and travel full-time, writing, speaking, and leading worship together. Brandi does professional life coaching and is a dog trainer, and believes that all dogs deserve a chance. The Cunninghams are based out of Texas and have eight dogs and incredible sons. They can be contacted at Firesidegrace@gmail.com.

Other Books by the Cunninghams

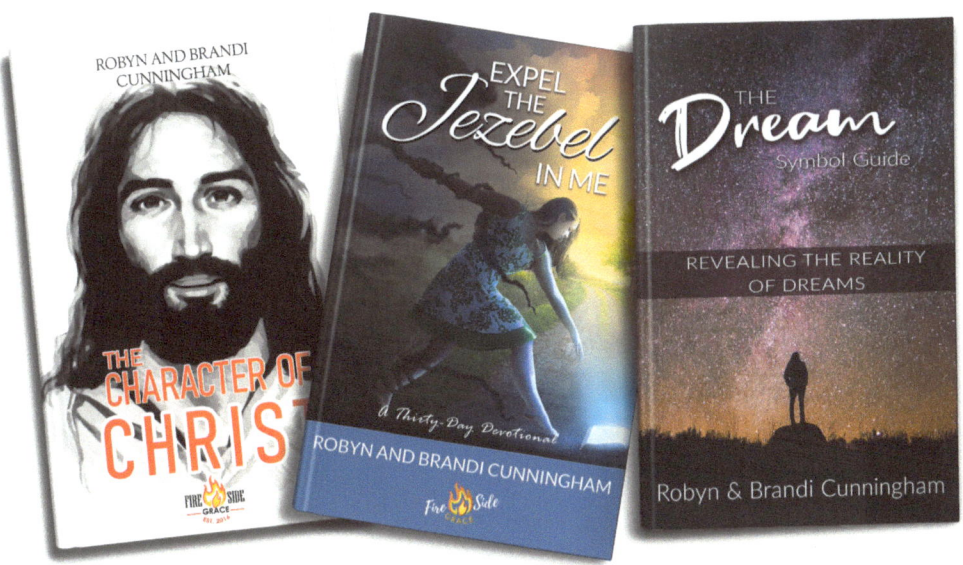

Find these great titles and more at www.FiresideGrace.com

www.ingramcontent.com/pod-product-compliance
Lightning Source LLC
Chambersburg PA
CBHW050752110526
44592CB00002B/45